Branded!

Introduction

Business Owners are greatly concerned about their Brand. This is happened as Marketing Professionals have done demonstrated the value of Branding in Business. The problem is that most of the examples given are premium brands of large companies. This kind of premium brand takes significant time and money to create. Most businesses can not afford the spending that it took to get Coca-Cola to be so powerful of a brand. This book is about what smaller businesses can do to define and grow their Brand.

A classical definition of brand might be as follows:

Unique design, sign, symbol, words, or a combination of these, employed in creating an image that identifies a product and differentiates it from its competitors. Over time, this image becomes associated with a level of credibility, quality, and satisfaction in the consumer's mind. Thus, brands help harried consumers in the crowded and complex marketplace, by standing for certain benefits and value. The legal name for a brand is a trademark and, when it identifies or represents a firm, it is called a brand name.

This definition is that it ignores what I think is the truly important part of Branding. That is the customer or prospect. Brand projection is important through all the visible mechanisms that companies and people use. The reason that this is the focus is that Brand from that perspective is under the control of the source of the Brand. But the value of the Brand is only in the eyes of the customer or prospect. This means that the Marketing Department does not have control over the value of its brand. All it can do is be the fountainhead of all the tangible aspects of the Brand.

This is my two part Definition of Brand as we start this book.

> **A Brand is:**
> **- Your Unique Value Proposition (UVP)**
> **- As Viewed in the Eyes of Your Customer or Prospect**

This means that the value of the Brand and its essence is how it is received and not in how it is presented. The presentation is important but the receipt is the fulcrum. The memory hooks that we use like Logos, Taglines and Names are all ways of reminding people of their relationship to your UVP. But it is the UVP that is most important. The goal is to link this UVP to the memory hook in such a way that the UVP is recalled even when it is unstated.

Now, why is this definition of Brand so challenging? Well, that is what we are going to explore over during this book. One last thing before we move on. Earlier, I talked about a Premium Brand. That is the goal of all Branding – to make the Brand itself have value and thus add value to the Business. The way that we will understand this will mean that it takes time and energy to create a Premium Brand. You can not start that way, but have to build to it.

Beyond that, my goal for this book is that it will provide you with thoughtful information about how to improve your Brand and make it work for you in your Business and your Life!

The View from the Customer Perspective

As I said, your Brand is your Unique Value Proposition in the Eyes of Your Customers and Prospects.

The first thing that I hope you understand is that this means it is not the messaging that you project but the messaging that is received that is important. Imagine some brands that have a strong connection like BMW or Apple. If you think about them they evoke a feeling about the company. Now do the same with BP. You get a feeling but it is not positive.

This ought to tell you the first point of Sales as it relates to Branding. Sales and Branding are emotional functions first and logical second. This has been studied many times and is part of the reason that works very strongly on their Branding message in Marketing.

The problem with that view is that Branding does not stop with Marketing. It starts there but does not end there. Everybody within the organization is responsible for Branding. Let me illustrate so you understand. Take a look at the BP logo. Did the Marketing team do a bad job on it? I don't think so. It has good colors and a symbolism with a flower design. The BP Brand issue is most notably what happened in the Gulf of Mexico. That had nothing to do with Marketing. But it is the value that we connect to the BP Brand.

So Brand has a lot more to do with the Execution of your Mission and Vision than it does with Logos and Letterhead. The latter is important but it is Execution of your Business that controls the outcome. This means that you need to connect all your employees with your Brand. Everybody in the business needs to know their part in the creation of your Brand.

Branding becomes a Whole Business affair because of this. This has 2 major implications. Your Brand's value is created by what you do. Start-up Businesses need to have Branding to create awareness of what they do. But a Start-up Brand has no value until the customers receive the products and services. This implies that a Premium Brand can only exist in an ongoing Business. A Startup should consider this content and put the correct perspective around Brand Development. The second implication is that your Brand is not the exclusive purview of Marketing. The Business Owner needs to be in charge of the Brand. The Business Plan needs to build the Business according to the Brand.   This is a 360 view of Branding and needs to involve everyone in the company.

Alignment

To grow a Brand you need to have a single concept down cold. That is Alignment.

This is one of the things I learned when being coached through the development of the 2001 Business Plan for Advanced Fibre Communications. If you all pull in the same direction all kinds of avenues in front of you open up. If you are pulling in different directions, you get nowhere. We used to say that you have to put all the wood behind the arrow. In our case, this was all about making sure that we wanted people to believe in the same things about the business.

We had one Executive in particular who wanted to pay lip service to our plan and then act in a completely different way. He used to perform a trust exercise to demonstrate that their trust needed to be placed with him and not others. What this created was a little pocket of pulling against the rest of us. This caused us to have great difficulty defining new releases as he kept wanting to add features and functions outside of the core market we were going after. Eventually our CEO investigated more deeply and the Executive was fired. But we lost about a year in trying to get ourselves moving forward rapidly.

I hope you see this lesson through this anecdote. But that is the point when you act in accordance with your Brand – you add to it. When you act contrary to your Brand – you subtract from it. Most Businesses spend time thinking about Brand Building. It seems odd that they would work against their own interests, but I hope I have given you some food for thought around how that happens.

What's funny is that most of the bad anecdotes start from a premise that makes some modicum of sense.

Very rarely does it happen that people screw things up on purpose. So, how does a company lose alignment? It has a lot to do with lack of Leadership. What? How did we get from an alignment in Branding to Leadership?

If you learn anything from this book, I hope is that "Actions speak Louder than Words" (or Logos). People associate your Brand with your Actions. How you inspire aligned actions from your Company? A Leader's job is to give people the fulcrum to make decisions. In any given day, we all make decisions about how to perform any given job. The job of Leadership is to tell people how we would like them to make these decisions. Then we hold people accountable for applying the principals that we have given them to their day to day work.

That is why Alignment is so important. If we are all making decisions based on the same criteria, then we will move in the same direction. This thought of Alignment can start from anywhere. I view the Business Plan as the place where it needs to be documented. Mission and Visions are required. But Business Plans are about Action. People need to know the Actions that they need to take to align themselves. The Business Plan is the place where the measurable are defined for people.

Alignment - Why it is the Key?

I want to take a step back and talk about why Alignment is the key to Branding and Business.

I always think we need to start with Goals. Any organization has to have Goals to achieve. What the Goals are is not important for the discussion. The thing to understand is that to reach your Goals, there will need to be action. I like to think of this as like a ship navigating. You need to move a ship through a set of waypoints. In order to move the ship, you have to put in energy. You have to change the direction. The bigger the ship the bigger the push required.

So, what does this have to do with alignment? Well, think of your business as that ship. You are navigating to your Goals. You need to push your business along to its goals. Is everything you and your team doing pushing with you? If not, then Alignment is the thing to look at. If people are pushing in the wrong direction, you may not meet your goals. The question is if you have people pushing the wrong way, what are you going to do about it?

Really it breaks into the problem of why people are pushing the wrong way. This can span the spectrum of knowledge, intention, and bull-headedness.

Knowledge is the easiest one to fix. Many times strategic thinking is not well explained up and down the chain of command. This causes people to do the wrong thing, thinking they are doing the right thing. Here it may be a question of extending the message all the way through the organization. It is critical that each Manager takes the higher level mission and extends it all the way to the bottom. You should be able to roll up the individual Goals of people and see that meeting them means that the company will hit its Goals. If this doesn't work, then we need to educate people on what they should be doing.

The intention is the next problem. Do people actively work against the Goals because they don't agree with them? I have seen that. The challenge can be either one of active sabotage because they want something different or because obtaining the Goal is bad for them personally. Either way, this kind of insidious behavior has to be quelled. That means that people have to be corrected and if they will not comply, then exited from the firm. There is simply no place for people that work actively against the company.

Finally, there is stubborn behavior. This is most often seen in parts of the company where the change is required. Many people are adverse to change and can create a drag on the company as it pursues its Goals. This is where Leadership is truly required. The employee is probably under the impression that he or she is doing the right thing. It will require a leap of faith by them to move to the next level and it is the job of leadership to get them there.

Alignment is what is going to drive your business like a ship to its Goals. Others may not be in alignment throwing you off course. This needs to be rectified and dealt with to make it to where you want to go.

Alignment and Communications

It's funny, I am listening to SportsCenter in the background as I type and they were talking about Alignment as it is applied to the Golden State Warriors. I think Alignment is the key to successful organizations and Sports Teams are the most visible way to see that.

But there is a part of Alignment that is paramount and that is Communications. The reason is that without Communications there can be no Alignment. You have to have a message that is both broad and narrow. The broad part of the message is that there needs to be a consistency for all your audiences. This can include employees, customers, partners, press, analysts, and shareholders. They should all be aware of the overall portions of your message. However, there will need to be specifics that relate to each audience. That part of your message must be narrow. That way the receiver of your message can find their connection to the message.

The primary group that you need to align is your employees. I talked about potential ways that people can not be aligned. Here is another part of the puzzle. How much direction do you give on alignment and how much freedom do you give people? A lot of the answer is simple. The more senior employees should have greater freedom. But it is a call that gets made with the individual and direct supervisor. Now that the path has been laid out, how do you want to contribute? There are clearly cases where this will need to be a directive effort, but by allowing the employee to participate they get to buy in. That buy-in will create a path for the employee to hold themselves accountable to their plan. If you provide the plan, then it is your plan. If you collaborate with an employee on a plan then it is a joint plan that both of you are responsible for.

The best part of a joint plan is that accountability is much easier to handle. No plan is going to work out perfectly, but if you collaborated on the creation of a plan then the employee can not back out of their portion of the responsibility for the plan. Now that may seem like it is a trick, but in fact, this is key. The reason that alignment is so important is that employees make thousands of decisions every day. They need a voice inside their head on how to weigh their choices with the goals that the company wants to meet. Without that voice, they may make a completely reasonable decision but one that heads in the wrong direction. If the plan that has been created is your plan, then the voice is your voice. A collaborative plan uses their voice as a guide. That makes the voice much more powerful.

You can use this collaborative process in any style of delegation. You would think that those that are being directed would not be a candidate for collaboration. In this case, the employee will have a set of choices outlined for them. The supervisor will have more regular checks on progress. But there is still a need for these low trust relationships to evolve and there is no better way than to do it than work on goals, plans and progress together.

Alignment and Customers

I think that internal communications are very important. Here I want to provide a thought about external communications. In particular, Communications with your Customers is critical.

Now most folks want to talk about Communications with new prospects and customers. I want to focus on the other end of the spectrum. Do you have an effective plan to communicate with your existing customers? Any Marketing or Salesperson worth their salt will tell you that it is easier to keep an existing customer than it is to land a new one.

I had a client that I was discussing their Unique Value Proposition (UVP) with a few weeks back and I posed the following question, "Have you asked your best customers why they hire you?" The intent of that question has a multitude of things that can be derived from it. In this case, the client was unclear on his UVP and I need to explore that with him. Since he has an ongoing and growing business, he is doing many things correctly. So, there is an academic exercise around Messaging that can be done. Why not find out what you are doing right already? Once he has talked to customers, he and I will sit down and see what he feels about the answers he has gotten.

This particular client works in a way that uses referral marketing with his client base. In fact, his business is built on that as a primary marketing channel. So, I asked him if he sends "Thank You" cards to his clients and includes a Business Card for them to hand out? The customer can see how important their business was and can give a card to a friend or neighbor that needs similar work done. This client is now implementing such a program with great success.

That is just one case and involves a particular client of mine. Everybody is different and needs to have a different communications plan with existing customers. The question that I have to ask you today is if you have looked at the alignment of these communications with your Brand and Messaging? It is just as important or perhaps more important than the messages that you send to your prospects. I saw a post that week that talked about Marketing Messaging on websites needed to be turned towards your existing customers. I disagree with that strongly. In many cases existing clients will not be visiting your website except to get phone numbers or location information. Specific customer offers they are likely on Landing Pages or Customer Portals that existing customers go to. Your main website is more a place for prospects than customers because of that.

So, in the end, it is pretty simple. Have you looked at your UVP and seen if your customer communications are in line with it? I am sure you have with your prospect communications. This might be the easiest way to grow your business. If you had a higher rate of customer retention or greater spending by return customers, it might be the best way to grow!

Alignment and Simplicity

One of the problems that I have seen with clients is that they often don't see the complexity of the messaging that they send out to their Customers, Prospects, and Partners. The complexity itself makes things difficult for others to see the value in their work.

So, how to fix it? Well, the starting point is the old Elevator Pitch. There is a lot of disdain for these short messaging formats. But in this context, it has a purpose, how to keep your message simple. The simpler and clearer what you say is the better off you are. If you need to make a long sales pitch, you have to ask yourself how differentiated you really are. If the benefits of what you do are that hard to understand, how much on top of the priority list will you be?

In case you don't know, an Elevator Pitch is what you might tell someone about your business in an Elevator ride. Generally, this is considered 1 minute or less with 3 ideas maximum to be communicated. Have you done this for your business? If not, it is the place to start. What would you do to communicate the important elements of your business in that short time what would you want your Customers, Prospects, and Partners to hear?

Once we have those messages, you can then look at the rest of your marketing with that message as the backbone of what your communications is. Does your marketing align with your Elevator Pitch? If not, why not? Get back to basics and communicate those primary messages first. Often times I see marketing material written for those that are already in the business that the client is in. The language that is used is "Inside Baseball". That means that people are confused on what is meant by what the material says. Clients are often not aware that they are doing it. This is a perspective thing. What is necessary is an Outside – In perspective. Think about your messaging from the perspective of the Customer. This is often a challenge for people that have worked in their business for a very long time. They can't get outside their box. In many ways, this is the best reason to engage outsiders. They can give you the perspective from outside the business without any prejudice, especially if they have not spent significant time within the industry.

So, even though that Elevator Pitch may never be actually used it becomes the best method of simplifying your message. There is one more element of this simplicity and that is repetition. People get your message through repeated contact. This is one of the primary goals of Alignment. Every contact that you have with a Prospect or Customer delivers the same message. Remember they are not inside your business every day to hear your message. They need to receive it regularly.

Alignment and Values

I write a lot about making sure that the messages that customers received were consistent and consistent with your Brand. I want to make sure that the message that is being communicated is an accurate reflection of your Brand.

Values are the key here. What do you believe about your business? What problems do you solve and how do you solve them? How do you make decisions? How do you deal with challenges and conflict? All of these questions and more come from a place of Value. The Value represents what you believe and how you act. It is this that people that you come in contact with will take away from any interaction. As it is said, Actions speak louder than Words.

So, how do you display your Values? You do so by being authentic in your communications and actions. People will react to authenticity. If you fake your way through conversations, that will come across to those you meet. It is why you can not overcome an objection that you believe in. Your prospects will see the truth and act accordingly.

So, when you build up your message you need to be authentic and bring your values to light in what you are doing. Almost any message can be made to work, but only your message will work for you. Bringing all of these elements together will naturally align your Brand with your Values. Of course, this gets to be a problem as you include other people whether they are employees, partners, prospects or customers. You will have much greater success with people that are aligned with your Values as well. This is why it is important to understand which Values are important to your work and workplace. Not every Value is important at work nor are they all worth bringing to the workplace. There are hot button topics that do not matter at work and it is fine to keep them separate. It does not mean that you should not have them, just that you need to be clear that they add nothing to your business.

This means that you should have a relatively short list of Values by which your business will operate. These need to be clear to everyone involved in it. The biggest challenge will be with employees and partners. They will often agree with your Values externally but not internally. There will be challenges that they present to your Values to see if they are true and authentic. It is at those moments where you get to decide whether these Values are real.

One of my past employers called together a management meeting at which we were told that the number one value of the company was being ethical. Within a week, I was told to evaluate a supplier and I let the team know that one of the senior members of the supplier was a convicted felon. I was then promptly told that this was not important and to continue the evaluation. As you can guess, I decided that being ethical actually did not matter to this company.

So, align your company with your values. Make sure your values are the way you want your business to run and then run it that way. This will build your Brand with all the people you meet.

Implementing Alignment

I have spent time focusing on Alignment as a topic in different aspects of your business. Essentially this is one of the core organizing principles in any business. I want to wrap up this topic giving you a view of the work involved in getting a mid-sized company aligned. This goes back to the completion of our 2001 Business Plan at AFC. We were about 1,000 employees and around $350M in revenue at that time.

The Business Plan itself took several months to go through. We were in a fundamental rethink of the business. We were doing fine, but much of the industry was collapsing around us. We took the time to step back and see what was going to happen. This strategic exercise changed the way we thought about many aspects of our business and ultimately led to our FiOS win at Verizon.

The problem was how to push all that change into 1,000 people to make sure that we were all pulling the same way. We announced the results of the planning process to the entire company. Then we brought the layer of management just below the C level in to run different task forces within the company. These task forces had an Executive sponsor but were run by a Director or a Vice President. Each of them had a specific focus and a broad-based team. The company and each team created dashboards that we read out at a quarterly review. There were about 10 of these teams and a quarterly review took a whole day.

Needless to say, this was an extensive commitment. It was imperfect in an implementation like all things. But we got it mostly right and the process made everyone buy into the plan. That alone was worth it. It makes it easy if everyone is pulling in the same direction.

There was a singular Executive who did not agree with this process and went his own way. Just one person like that was a weight in the room. He bent the rules to get what he wanted and it hurt the cohesion of the team and the process. Eventually, he was let go and things improved dramatically. His goal was not the success of the plan but instead the growth of his own influence. That kind of person exists in almost every organization of any size. Senior managers have to be looking out for them and root them out of organizations. They simply don't work in teams and that is what alignment is all about.

I personally tried to model the opposite behavior. I tell people that much of my job at the time was what I called "Executive without Portfolio". By that I mean, I would often be brought in as a temporary leader to fix and organization. Then, I would hire my replacement. The goal was to bring in an expert to replace me so that the team was stronger when I was done running an organization. That way I tried to show how to build an organization without building an empire. When I see empire building it is not a good sign.

So, Align your Business and Your Brand. It is the key to success.

Brand Message

Many of the smaller businesses that I work with have particular trouble with getting a really clear Brand Message. What I find is a lot of companies are having a difficult time differentiating them and fall into the category of commodity. There is some fear that associates with being a commodity and the inability to build an effective business. Here I am going to start with my definition of a Brand Message.

So, there are lots of bits to Branding. As you have read, I don't place a huge amount of stock directly in the older notions of Branding like logos and taglines. I am not saying that these have no value nor do I think they are unimportant. But I want these to be a result, not a cause. By that I mean that to me the most important thing is to understand the message and how you will propagate it. The devices that you attach to the message as a memory tool are of secondary significance.

So what exactly is a Brand Message?

It is the communication of the reason and emotion that you want your prospects to feel when they consider buying your products and services.

Remember Selling is an emotional process first backed up by reason. To put this in context, you need to describe to your customer how they should feel when they have bought your Brand. After that, you need to provide reasons for them to agree with this feeling and process it internally.

I used to work for a company named Advanced Fibre Communications (AFC). For a long time, AFC let the small carriers in the US (the IOCs) know that they were very important to the company. It did so by many actions that were made to order to support that community. AFC had small carrier specific events all across the year and had internal organizations designed specifically to support them. It made sure that the product designs met the needs of the IOCs. If you look back into the history of Carrier Access, you can find how this impacted AFC in other markets. This activity created a lot of good feeling in both directions in an (at the time) underserved market. That bred success and differentiation.

So, I want to explore how to create, understand, and execute your Brand Message and help you have that same kind of success.

Brand Message – How to Start

My definition of a Brand is your Unique Value Proposition (UVP) as viewed by your Ideal Prospects and Clients. That last bit is very important as I view a Brand as actionable. Your Brand is only as good as your execution against what your promise is. And that promise is your Brand Message.

Let me create a circle of this idea again so that you can see how it fits together. You define your UVP to describe what is important about what you do. You describe your Ideal Client to be clear on who your target audience is. You write your Brand Message as a promise about your Products and Services. You execute your UVP to deliver on your promise. When you do this, it builds your Brand.

This leads to the first problem that I run into when talking to Businesses. The Brand Value is only as good as your weakest link. In a Small Business, the weakest link is Execution. You can use Your Brand Message anything you want and if you can't deliver then it has no value. Actions speak louder than words and so Execution wins the day. Think about bad service at a Restaurant and how it colored your entire experience of the place. The food may have been wonderful, but you still are not going back.

But we are focused on your Brand Message here. That implies a couple of things. The first thing is that you make a promise to your Prospect. That is a promise of Value. The question you should put behind your Brand Message is: "Is my Value promise meaningful to my Ideal Prospects and Clients?" I have seen plenty of Brand Messages that do not resonate with the only group that matters – those that are paying the bills.

Finally on this topic, I want to come back to Alignment. Because Execution is such a big piece of the puzzle, you need to have all of your Team on board with your Brand Message. Otherwise, delivery of your promise doesn't happen and your Brand loses Value.

Your Action is to figure out what that promise you are making to your prospects. And then make the promise a reality when the prospects become customers.

Brand Message – Bringing it to Life

We recognize that your Brand Message is all about the Value Promise to your Prospects and Customers. The Execution of that Brand Message is what your Customers attach themselves to. Today's post is all about how we create Brand Recognition.

Brand Recognition is all about creating an Audience for your Brand. This means that before you have any Human Interaction with your Prospects that they have knowledge of what you do. It would be even better if your Brand conveyed to them some type of Value at that level, but this may or may not be true. Here is the problem. The large Brands we see today (especially in the Consumer Markets) spend large sums of money for this activity. Small Businesses do not have the kinds of capital to Execute the same strategy. What can be done?

Well, the first place to start is the definition of your Ideal Client. The reason is that the resources you are going to spend need to get spent effectively. The best way to spend those dollars is to focus them on the Prospects that will deliver you the most value. One of the problems for many Small Businesses is that they want this pool to be as large as possible. The owners reason that getting as many Prospects as possible will give them the best chance to close business.   A more efficient way is to understand who you want to sell to and target your Brand at those Prospects as a priority.

The second point is to review your Brand Message and the promise that it makes. Does the promise have Value in the eyes of your Ideal Client? This is something very important and needs to be looked at from the outside in. One of the challenges that many businesses have is that they view their Value as they project it. Remember, it is the Prospect that has to perceive the value from the message. Remember that as you bring your message to the marketplace.

Third, you need to be consistent with the way your Brand Message is presented. This is the whole connection to your Logo, Colors, and Tagline. The entire point of Audience creation is to have a number of touch points by which you reach out to potential Prospects. What the traditional Branding elements are intended to do is reinforce your Brand Message so that the appearance of one of the Branding elements causes recall of the Brand Message. One of the most important parts of this is consistency. Every time your Brand is seen or heard you want consumers to connect it to your Brand Message. This works best if the visual and audio representation of your Brand is constant.

So, that is a great way to start thinking about how to bring your Brand Message to Life.

Brand Message – The 4 Quadrants

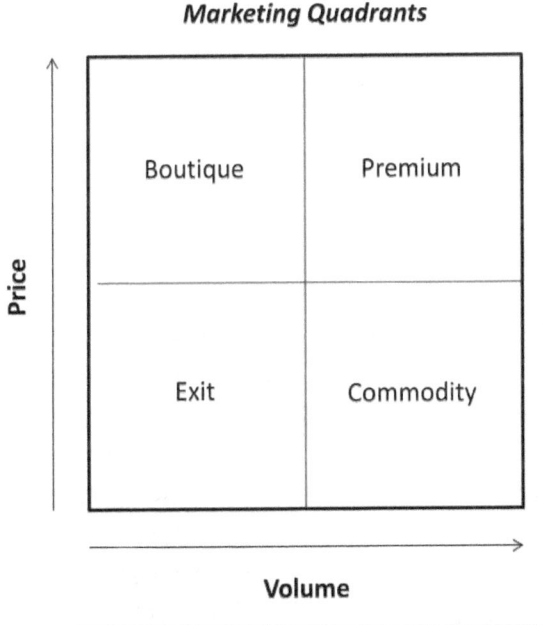

Marketing Quadrants

It is important to understand how to Brand a product based on how you are building your Business. The goal for all businesses is to push where they lie up and to the right. But especially before you have Branded, you are not likely to be able to command a price premium for your products and services.

In general, it is easier to create a Boutique Brand than expand one that is a Commodity. The way to start with a Boutique Brand is to focus the message that creates that premium value to a target market. This means the only expense is the cost to change messaging. Generally to expand a commodity market, it requires broader advertising costing more money.

Brand Message - The Boutique Brand

As I advise companies to create a Boutique Brand, they often find that they have an existing market position closer to the Exit point. So how do we get started?

I have to go over with folks in this position is how to get out of the low pricing that they have done in the past without upsetting any existing customers. I ask them to do two things. The first thing is to make sure that services are all enumerated on any invoices, even if they are going to be discounted to zero. This makes sure that existing customers understand that they have been getting a discounted price and they have gotten a lot more value than they paid for. In order to make this look more normal, I suggest a "Partner Program". This way existing customers can be defined as Partners and the discounts can be defined. You can use that same Partner Discount if you want in the future if you want. These customers see retail price and understand they are getting a good deal. The point of these activities is to get the pricing built to match the value and not discounted to the bottom.

After that, we begin working on how to define their unique value and ideal client. There is generally another round of nervousness when we go back to the ideal client. I have to fight the desire to go back to a broad definition of ideal customers. But once we are past that, we get into defining their unique value. One of the challenges that I have to remind customers about is that this is about Branding. The message that I drive relentlessly is that your Brand is **"Your Brand is your Unique Value Proposition in the eyes of your Ideal Client."** It requires that the Business is focused on the viewpoint of the Client. Many people don't easily reformat their thinking to take a client viewpoint. Once we go around all of this a couple of times, it is time to reformat their Business Plan based on this new methodology.

The change in Business Plan needs to reflect the changes in the number of clients that a Boutique Brand will have and the profit from each of them. This is going to be very different than the plan that would be used for low-value transactions. This is especially true of Advertising expenditures. We will talk about the materials around this in the future. But one thing to think about is that now you are talking about a very specialized audience. Do they find their vendors in the same place as the more general audience?

It is critical that all the parts of the Brand as it is distributed add to the Boutique Brand Value.

Brand Message - What About Commodities?

What happens if you decide not to build a boutique brand but instead focus on being a commodity? There is nothing wrong with being a commodity. Your company can do very well as such a player, but it does provide some messaging differences for Branding.

To start, the easiest thing to do is to think about what is known as being "Cheap and Cheerful". That means a no frills approach to doing business. This does not imply poor quality product, just something that doesn't have bells and whistles. If I look at cars for a second, imagine a car today without power windows. You don't NEED power windows but most models have them. And it keeps going. Imagine your car without the extras. No power seats, no power steering, no automatic transmission, and no power brakes. That was the base model of every car when I was a kid. Heck, even a Radio and Seat Belts cost extra. Because the models we examine have the extras, we don't tend to look at the costs imposed.

Let me run you some cost numbers, I have gotten into recently. My son wondered if I wanted a Keurig machine to replace my coffee maker. I am a big coffee drinker and I had thought about this many times. Well, I went to a store and found that K-cups in my local Safeway goes for around $0.70 each. I did some Googling and some math and found 12-oz bag coffee ran me about $0.23 a cup. So, Keurig has done a GREAT job of building a boutique brand. But I looked at those numbers and thought that I would keep my existing coffee maker. However, I do want to point out that a mid-sized Starbucks Coffee (a Grande) goes for just over $2.00 a cup. Makes you think about how you are spending your money on coffee eh?

Having all the essentials is the point of a Commodity Brand. Why am I spending all that money on frills? Do I really need or want a Nordstrom experience when I just want to buy Underwear? Can I get a good value for them at Target? So, when you build a commodity it is all about delivering solid value at a good price. You will sell more volume than your Boutique Competition, but your profit per sale will be lower. This means you have to be ruthless about cost across the board. This is especially true when it comes to Marketing and Advertising.

So, being a commodity is all about being good at the things you do and not being great for a small number of people.

Brand Message - Ads and Targeting

I asked the question if the Boutique Customers for your specialized (Boutique) products and services look for them in the same place as the General Customer.

This is one of the big advantages of the Boutique Brand. The more specific of an audience you are addressing the easier they are to promote your products and services to. They will generally have some very particular ways that they search for vendors. By marketing your products and services in these venues then you will most directly connect to your customers. By placing your Branding Message in front of the people that are most likely to buy your products then you have done the best that you can in generating interest and leads for your business.

What this means is that you are wasting as little resources as you can on prospects who are not likely purchasers. There is an old adage that "50% of your advertising spend is wasted, the problem is you can't tell which 50% it is." Well, here we are trying to minimize that waste. This is important because Lead Generation is the most expensive activity in Marketing to grow. It is much less expensive to improve your Lead Conversion (the percentage of Leads that become Customers). But this focus also improves your Lead Conversion as you are generating leads for your business that are more likely to be buyers.

This leads us back to our Brand Message. Take a look at your Marketing Materials and Advertisements and make sure that they are aligned with Your Brand Message. If you remember Your Brand Message is the promise made to a prospect. So your advertising placement needs to align with the values of Your Brand Message. You want to ensure alignment to make sure that your prospects get a consistent message.

Finally, we need to talk about pricing and discounting. If you are executing a Boutique Brand, then you need to be above average on pricing. This is because you will have targeted a portion of the market that you are satisfying completely. They will end up desiring your products as they are the best fit. Commodity Brands should go for lower than average pricing or at least be able to have a business with relatively low pricing. Even though you will have lower gross margins, by upping volume it will be the goal to overwhelm the fixed costs in your Business.

This leads us to a conversation on discounting. Coupons are only appropriate for Commodity Brands as they offer no differentiation. If you want to discount, then see if there is a partner program that you can create. This way you can adjust pricing to customers if you want, but keep that discounting in a one on one format. So, you can discount – just don't go into a broadcast mode with it. If you want a bit of a broader approach, then try a loyalty card. This targets repeat customers but does not add value to new customers.

Brand Message - In Practice

I had a couple of opportunities recently to discuss Branding with clients. I thought it might be useful to talk about real world challenges that Small Business Owners face. Both of these examples come from my view that Brand and Brand Messaging has to do with Execution in the Business.

The first example comes from a firm in the Marketing Business. This is a Business owned by a Couple and they are the primary actors in the Business. We are working on re-positioning the Business to serve a higher end clientele. The challenge is that the most technical of the partners comes from a background and experience that is contrary to the kind of Brand they want to develop. This has caused some customer confusion and loss of potential business. I wanted to give them some concrete steps on how to make a change.

As usual, I fell back to Automobile companies. They make such wonderful examples in Branding because of the variety and breadth of examples. I asked the person to describe to me someone dispatched from the company to deal with a car issue. In one case, the car was a Rolls-Royce. In the other, it was a VW Bug. He gave a description of the different people that would show up. I pointed out to him that neither was right or wrong. They simply were and that is okay. The two people they described were very different and we talked about the differences.

Next, I asked them about some companies that they respected in their business. I got some answers and asked how my clients differed and how they wanted to work within their business and what image they wished to project. I think the client got it at that point. They get to project any image that they choose. But they do get to choose it and they need to be consistent about it.

The outcome of all of this was that the client has started landing large jobs from bigger customers. This is exactly what we wanted to have happened so that the couple could grow the business effectively. They still do smaller jobs as fill-in work, but their main goal is to attract larger clients through their direct marketing. This program has been a great success.

Later, I met a client in the Construction Business. They had the problem that many of the employees did not demonstrate the same values that they did. We talked about that. I started by suggesting that he make sure that all the employees know what his differentiation is. T his is all part of his Brand Message to prospects and clients. If his employees are not clear on the Brand, then they need to be as they are customer facing on a regular basis. We went through the exercise of going from the Lead Generation from following through on the Brand Message all the way to their paychecks.

This helped his employees understand how they were viewed by the customers. He was able to help his employees to understand how he wanted them to act on a job site. We set up a program to regularly remind employees of how they were supposed to work with customers. This has greatly improved his customer retention and referral rate.

I hope seeing Branding and the Brand Message in action helps. Everybody has challenges and with just a bit of effort, we can make things much clearer and better for our customers.

The 7 Ps of Marketing

Up to this point, I have taken what I think of as a pass through the Business as how one might think of it logically when one is looking at developing a Brand. Here I want to describe Branding as it relates to a standard view of Marketing. In this case, I am using the 7 Ps.

This model is called a Marketing Mix and work first started on this type of Model in the 1960s. Even with its existence, many people outside of Marketing do not grasp the model. I am utilizing the extended model that was created to help include Services Business.

The 7 Ps are:

1. *Product*
2. *Pricing*
3. *Place*
4. *Promotion*
5. *People*
6. *Process*
7. *Physical Evidence*

My plan is to look at each of these elements and describe provide a story about each of them and how they can impact your Brand. The goal is to help give you a 360-degree look at a Business from a Marketing standpoint and link it to how that can build or destroy your Brand.

Branding - Product

As we start our journey through the 7 Ps of Marketing. The first of the elements to examine is Product. This is the core of any offering. It is also the place that potentially the largest Branding mistake of all time comes from.

Let me start with an example from my career. When I started at Advanced Fibre Communications (AFC), we primarily served the smallest of Telephone Companies in the US. We built our company in such a way to serve this market. Many functions contributed, the UMC-1000 itself was designed to serve these customers well. In fact, some of these same capabilities were a problem for the largest of the Telephone Companies.

So, you can see already that we had built our Brand as one that served smaller customers in the US. We did this through the execution of our product. This allowed AFC to obtain a huge market share within that customer base. However, this also limited our ability to sell to larger customers. Other companies have followed that same model since that time. But I hope it is evident that our Logo did not set the standard for this, it was the way we built our Product and Business. The early customers were attached to the company in such a way that they did not call the product the UMC or UMC-1000. They would just call it "The AFC".

This kind of execution led to the market share and profitability which funded later expansion.

But one needs to look no further than Product to see the largest Branding disaster of all time: "New Coke". If you are young, you may not remember this. Coke and Pepsi had been fighting the Cola Wars for decades. With Coke changing its formula, the folks at Pepsi were able to state that Coke had essentially surrendered to the better product by trying to copy it. The idea may have been interesting, but there were a lot better ways to execute it as a business. There has been a lot written about this if you just Google it you will find all kinds of information about this event.

I thought it might be interesting to put out a more interesting example: the Porsche 914. Porsche is a high-end performance brand. It worked with Volkswagen to build an entry level model. VW was best known for the original Beetle model. Consumers knew this and found it confusing that the entry level car company was working with a performance car company. The 914 was never to be confused with the performance models and thus diluted the value. On the other hand, the 914 allowed more people to own a Porsche than ever before. So, you could see this as a potentially mixed experience. In the long term, there has been no damage nor any benefit to the Brand. But it is something to think about seriously.

If I use just that last example, think of the marketing implications. If you are an owner of say a Porsche 911, do you really want to have the name associated with the VW Beetle? Porsche owners were interested in the racing heritage of the Brand. Before you dilute your product offering, think on this question.

Branding - Pricing

Now we get to talk about Price.

I want to start with a pretty simple question for all of you. Do you attend Workshops? What does the pricing of the Workshop do in your thinking around it? I can tell you that my experience is that people attend at the highest rate those workshops that have a modest fee. Why is that?

Too high of a price is easy to explain. Unless the speaker is well known or the topic is completely relevant, the value of the time spent is too rich. This means that too high of a price drives away people who have no Brand Awareness or have low Brand Value.

On the other hand, Free can be just as troublesome. Having a free activity means that you have told the attendee that there is Low Value. You did this whether you meant to or not. The attendee will register and only attend if they have nothing to do.

This examination brings us back to our optimal pricing of some nominal fee. You have told the person that you are giving them value but not pricing it so high that they won't risk an hour of their time. Having this sort of pricing has told people about the Value that you are bringing. There will be some Value in the topic, but expect to have a Call-To-Action (CTA) for further purchases. This kind of CTA is expected and acceptable as long as it does not get obnoxious.

So, now we can take a step back and see what our Pricing of this single item has done. It has defined the Value that should be expected. Attendees can then decide whether they place the same worth on what you have delivered as you do. Meeting and preferably exceeding Price and Value builds your Brand. People who are buying either high price or low price are comparing their purchase with Expected Value ahead of time and Actual Value after purchase. By providing more than the Expected Value, you build your Brand.

This is what Brand Value. Did the Customer think he or she got more than what she paid for? You have two variables: The Price and the Product/Service. The Customer will then report his or her experience to others. This comparison and the subsequent conversation is where Brand ultimately gets built.

Branding - Place

I think people have a better feel for Place as a customer than they do as a Business Owner. One of the ways I have seen this is when I watch "Restaurant Impossible".

If you have ever watched the show owners call in a gentleman named Robert Irvine. Robert and a team rebuild a restaurant in 2 days. About 80% of the time, the decor is one of the big issues. Well, I should back up and say that the "Place" is a big issue. It seems to be a pattern that bad restaurants have cleanliness issues on his show. Not all the time, but most of the time. Now if you walk into a restaurant and it smells bad, what do you think as a customer? Something is wrong. The same is true if you look around and there are filthy carpets, dusty blinds, and general clutter.

This is where Place comes into your Brand. I work out of my home as do many people in my business. The majority of my meetings happen at my client offices. Some of them happen to coffee shops and the rest happen on-line. I get to travel to see where people work. And that first impression makes a difference. That is why Marketing folks put such an emphasis on logos, signage, website design, and colors.

But the quality of your office space and location of it makes a difference. We have a high-end Steakhouse in town that is in a relatively bad neighborhood. I have seen needles in the parking lot while I was walking in.

This does not provide a good feeling as someone who is planning to spend $50/head for dinner. I am surprised that this location was chosen and they have stayed there. I have certainly been hesitant to take clients to this restaurant.

So, you can see how this all plays together as part of your brand. What people want and expect is that the location is convenient and safe. They want the style to represent you and yours. If it doesn't then they are disappointed with your company and it hurts your Brand. None of this has to be fancy or overdone. Unless you are a fancy and overdone brand as a choice that is. Simple can work just fine. It all depends on expectations.

I like to use Hotels as a good way to think about it. Now, you can imagine that a Motel 6 and the Ritz-Carlton are going to be very different. But we can go further and look at others in each of those price classes. The Ritz is known for opulence. But imagine staying at a "W" Hotel. Look them up if you want. They are supposed to be trendy and fashionable. Would you expect the Ritz to be the same? The Ritz is more Opulent and more Old World. The W is more Sleek Black and Chrome.

Both can work and have markets. But put the W's music in the Ritz and it would be a big branding mistake!

Branding - Promotion

It's funny. I actually started this working on this topic is because of something that happened to me in this category. I received a ValPak. For those not familiar with this, it is a mailed group of Coupon type advertisements that come once a month or so. I opened mine up and thumbed through the pages. One of the ads struck me oddly. It was for a high-end pet salon.

Now, what is wrong with a Coupon here? Branding. Now, I get the idea – let's generate some new revenue. But ValPak's indicate low-end commodity goods. I am not trying to demean a ValPak or their advertisers, but I would not expect a Tiffany ad in one. See the point? I am talking about a high-end pet salon. When I went to their website, they touted their experience. The text on the site leads one to understand that they are taking the maximum care of your pet.

And then they send out an ad right next to the Smog Testing companies. I hope I have been repetitive enough about this now. You need to make sure that the way you promote your products and services enhance your brand.

A great example of proper promotion comes to me via my friends at Fuzeviewer. They worked with the local BMW dealer on a promotion for a brand new BMW model. There was only going to be one made available for the dealer and they decided to sell it in an interesting way.

The dealer did a direct mailer that allowed the user to scan with the Fuzeviewer app. As part of this, the user could enter a bid on the car. The car sold at list price and money above that were donated to charity. I hope you can see how this created exclusivity for the BMW dealer and brand. On top of that, service to the community was made front and center. This is just doing things the right way.

So, as you are thinking about your promotions you have go beyond just looking for where your customers are looking for your products. You need to understand each element of the promotion and see if it enhances your brand. Where is the promotion taking place? What is the Call To Action? How will existing customers react? How will new customers react? By getting the answers to align with your Brand builds value.

Branding - People

Alignment is a major theme of what I talk about with Branding. I want to be clear about the major reason that Alignment is so important – the People at your company.

Before I get on to the main point of the topic, I want to remind you that the People involved include not just your employees but the people you surround yourself with. This includes advisors, vendors, and customers. As I go through this topic, I want you to think about all of these folks.

When I talk about Alignment, I work to make sure that you understand that everything that you do is related to everything else. The front line of that element of Branding is the people that work for you. As I have stated in the past, it is the full view of your actions by your customers that makes your Brand. Many of these actions are performed by your employees.

Think about the last time you had bad service at a Restaurant. It can spoil an excellent meal that takes place in a wonderful atmosphere. I think that this should give you all you need to know. One bad waiter or waitress can cause many customers never to return.

As a Leader, you have three obligations. First and foremost, is to hire well. This is not a skill that is taught often today. I think the last time I went to a hiring and interviewing class was the late-80s. I know that we under-train our leaders as the advance in their careers, but this problem seems odd to me. We all know that People are very important. But we spend no time and money helping people to understand how to locate the right ones.

The second obligation of a Leader is to tell people how you want them to how to make decisions. The whole point of Leadership is to set direction. Every day your employees make decisions. As a Leader, you can not direct each decision personally. Your job is to tell your employees how you would make the decision if you were doing it. What factors you would weigh. What is important and what is not. If you do this properly, the People will use their judgment to add value to your Brand.

The third obligation of a Leader is to hold people accountable. Once you have told people how you want them to make decisions, you need to hold them accountable for the decisions that they make. That means that they get rewarded when they do things right. It also means that they are corrected when they do things wrong. If you don't correct problems they fester and impact other people. The rest of the staff will see the gap that is created between what you asked people to do and what they actually do. If you don't hold people accountable to their tasks, then everyone else will expect that they can not meet their obligations as well.

All of this is to help people understand what people need to do to support your Brand. Their actions will be what people know about your business. It is important that you and your people need to be in Alignment with your Brand.

Branding - Process

The next of the 7 Ps is Process. Process is a difficult one to describe, so I will give an example from my past. In this case, we will talk about processes that are externally facing. There are challenges in making sure the way a company works internally as well is aligned but each firm works differently.

In this case, I want to draw on my experience from Red Condor. The week I arrived, the company was releasing a new version of the product. It failed on release in a way that created a large number of issues for many different subscribers. One of the problems was that the Test Department did not have an effective test for that particular issue. The cost to develop one was very large. But the problem was really a process problem. This Process problem created a Market/Branding problem as the company's reputation for quality and performance was damaged.

So, let me back up a second and talk about the market challenge at Red Condor. The company started by providing SaaS solutions to small businesses and local governments for Spam Filtering. This became problematic to scale and there were inconsistent marketing methods applied to the scaling. At that point, the market focus was moved to small ISPs. These customers were larger and brought more subscribers in a single sale. Where an Enterprise sale might bring 1,000 users, an ISP sale brought 10s of 1000s.

The issue with serving these different markets is that the feature sets and the requirements of the two markets are not the same. This was particularly true around Customer Service. ISPs were used to having their own people provide maintenance for products and had some challenges using a SaaS solution because of this. Again, not a universal issue but it did mean that we had to up our game on the service side.

So, how did this all become a Process and Branding issue? Given the financial plight of Red Condor at the time, we decided to separate out the releases between the ISPs and the smaller businesses. It was a calculated risk that losing 1 or two small customers on a new release was less painful than losing an ISP. Not a great solution, but one that cost no money to implement. Given that we were teetering on bankruptcy, it was a path forward.

From a Branding Standpoint, what it meant was that we were more about the ISPs over time than we were about the Small Business Customers. Of course, the customers saw this, and the expansion of the SMB business slowed.

The ISP business picked up rather dramatically over the next couple of years and it was a tradeoff that you had to make.

There are lots of ways that companies signal what they think about the markets that they serve and how the customers react to that. In this case, our Process changes led directly to how our Brand was perceived by the two different customer bases that we had. Something to think about as you change things!

Branding – Physical Evidence

The last of the 7Ps came into the discussion as Branding extended from Product Companies to Service Companies. With a product, there is certainly evidence of Branding in the design and operation of the Product. Services often provide an intangible benefit. This means that the opportunities for Branding are less distinct. This is a problem in my own Business.

One of the Services that I offer is targeted at Small Business Owners particularly those that do not have a little formal business education. I present this to the world as a Training Class that is mixed with consulting specific to the individual. It is intended as an entry-level offering, with some opportunity to get some referrals out of it.

So, what did I do? I produced a Completion Certificate. As it is a "Class", I produced a Graduation. It gave me a chance to reconnect with the clients and provide them with Physical Evidence of the Class. On top of that if the Certificate is displayed, then I can get a chance to get some additional recognition. The main thing is that it all has to be classy so that it builds value into the Brand.

Whether it is certificates or swag or bags, make sure that you can add value to what you do through connecting people with Physical Evidence of your Products and Services. Just like everything else that you do, people will judge your Brand by how you execute it!

Branding in the Internet Age

There are several things to consider about Branding as we push Businesses into the Age of the Internet. The Internet does many wonderful things and one of them is that it is a great way to build your Brand. All the general rules hold for Branding. That includes things like the quality of your Website and the way your Brand Message is presented. There are three specific areas to think about when it comes to Branding and the Internet

The first of the three issues is Content and Content Marketing. My big beef with the way people treat their Brand on the Internet is the use of poorly conceived Content Marketing. I am a big believer in Content. But having a site filled with blog posts that are designed to fulfill the requirements of Search Engine Optimization (SEO) is not real Content. That is what I want you to think about here.

Most Businesses do not write most or all of their Blog posts or their Social Media posts. They outsource the work to 3rd parties. To me, this is all a question of the Brand and the Values it represents. For me, this would not work. I am all about Education and Learning. I do share 3rd party articles that I think are good, but I generate a lot of content myself.

Another part of this challenge out there related to content is balanced on your website. If you have multiple products and services, remember to treat them all fairly. I see so many sites that are dominated by one or two of the Products and Services that are offered. This makes you wonder if the other Products are important. There is a message that is being sent if you spend a lot of time one thing and not another.

So, think about the Content that you are generating and see that it makes sense and helps not just your SEO but your Brand. SEO is great for today but your Brand is great for a Lifetime.

The second of these issues is E-mail and E-mail Marketing. Do you cold call via E-mail? Depending on what you do and how you do it, E-mail Marketing can be very effective. Spamming people with requests to sell them something on an ongoing basis can be very detrimental to your Brand. As with Content, be sure of what you are doing and why you are doing it. If you are building a high-value Brand, do not take low-value actions and tarnish it.

Finally, there is the problem of Online Reputation. This is a truly double-edged sword. Online Reputation on sites like Yelp! can be very powerful as they help people choose products and services. The problem is that these sites are imperfect as all reviewing systems are. People can generate false positive and negative reviews. There is little that can be done to change this. The one thing that you can do is respond to criticism in a positive way. Evaluate negative reviews and see if the comment is fair. If it is, then offer something to the poster. If the commentary is not fair do not argue with the person. There is nothing good that happens when you do. Just realize that all of your competitors are in the same environment and can receive unfair poor reviews as well.

Wrapping it all up!

Branding is a huge topic that can be studied for years. This is intended to introduce Branding in a way that provides help to Business Owners and Executives on how to make their Brand work for them

I want to walk back through a bit of what we should remember about Branding. Let's start with our definition:

> **A Brand is:**
> **- Your Unique Value Proposition (UVP)**
> **- As Viewed in the Eyes of Your Customer or Prospect**

Looking back up the chain of logic, this means that you must be clear on both Your UVP and Your Ideal Client. Without understanding these two items, you are likely to have a problem in creating Your Business. You will spend resources trying to sell products and services to prospects that are not the best fit. Remember, it is those Ideal Prospects that you are going to spend money on attracting them to your Business.

The outside-in viewpoint is paramount here and represents the most important way to build your Brand:

Align the Execution of Your Business with the Values of Your Brand.

This is where Business Execution comes into focus. Are you and your employees meeting the Brand Promise every time? If not, then you have to change that. This is what Brand building in the real world is all about. Meeting and exceeding the expectations of your customers. You made them specific promises and now it is time to follow through on them. That is what will build your reputation and your Brand.

Remember that your Brand conveys your Brand Promise:

The Brand Promise is the communication of the reason and emotion that you want your prospects to feel when they consider buying your products and services.

So when we think about Taglines and Logos, think about the message that is being conveyed about you and your Business. Does your promise reflect the reality of your Business? Are you clear how your actions help your Brand?

One way to be clear is to view your Business through the lens of the 7Ps of Marketing. That is a straightforward way to think about your Brand and your Business. Many of the anecdotes that I provided should help guide you through an examination of your own Business.

What you do now is up to you. But you can make your Business stronger by building your Brand. The right time to take action is today!